A Practical Guide to Early Years Matters

Volume 1

By FLORENCE O. AJALA

This book is dedicated to all those who are willing to positively impact young children's lives.

Do you want to promote holistic development in young children?

Do you need the skills to manage the challenging behaviour of young children?

Do you want to develop mathematical skills in young children?

Do you want to develop independence in young children?

Do you want to promote diversity in early childhood?

If yes, then this book is for you. This book is a practical guide with a rationale for supporting young children's learning and development around the world. The period from birth to eight years are critical and formative years, and it is important that young children are supported to reach their developmental milestones during these years. This book is predominantly aimed at parents, guardians, and teachers of young children from birth to eight years to offer appropriate and evidence-based support.

There is a lot of information in the public domain about young children's learning and development; however, much of it is factual, rather than practical. In this book, I will share various practical and useful approaches to supporting young children's learning and development.

Florence O. Ajala, BA Early Childhood Care and Education, Grad Dip Education, Doctoral Researcher in Reflective Pedagogy and Early Childhood Studies, is a teacher and trainer in Early Childhood Studies based in the Republic of Ireland. She creates content on early Childhood learning and development for her  YouTube Channel and Facebook Page (Early Years Matters TV). She is keen on promoting young children's learning and development.

'Education is the most powerful weapon, which you can use to change the world.' (Nelson Mandela)

'The years of early childhood are the time to prepare the soil,' (Rachel Carson)

'Children are like wet cement. Whatever falls on them makes an impression,' (Dr. Hiam Ginnot)

'Education is a natural process carried out by the child and is not acquired by listening to words but by experiences in the environment,' (Maria Montessori)

Table Of Contents

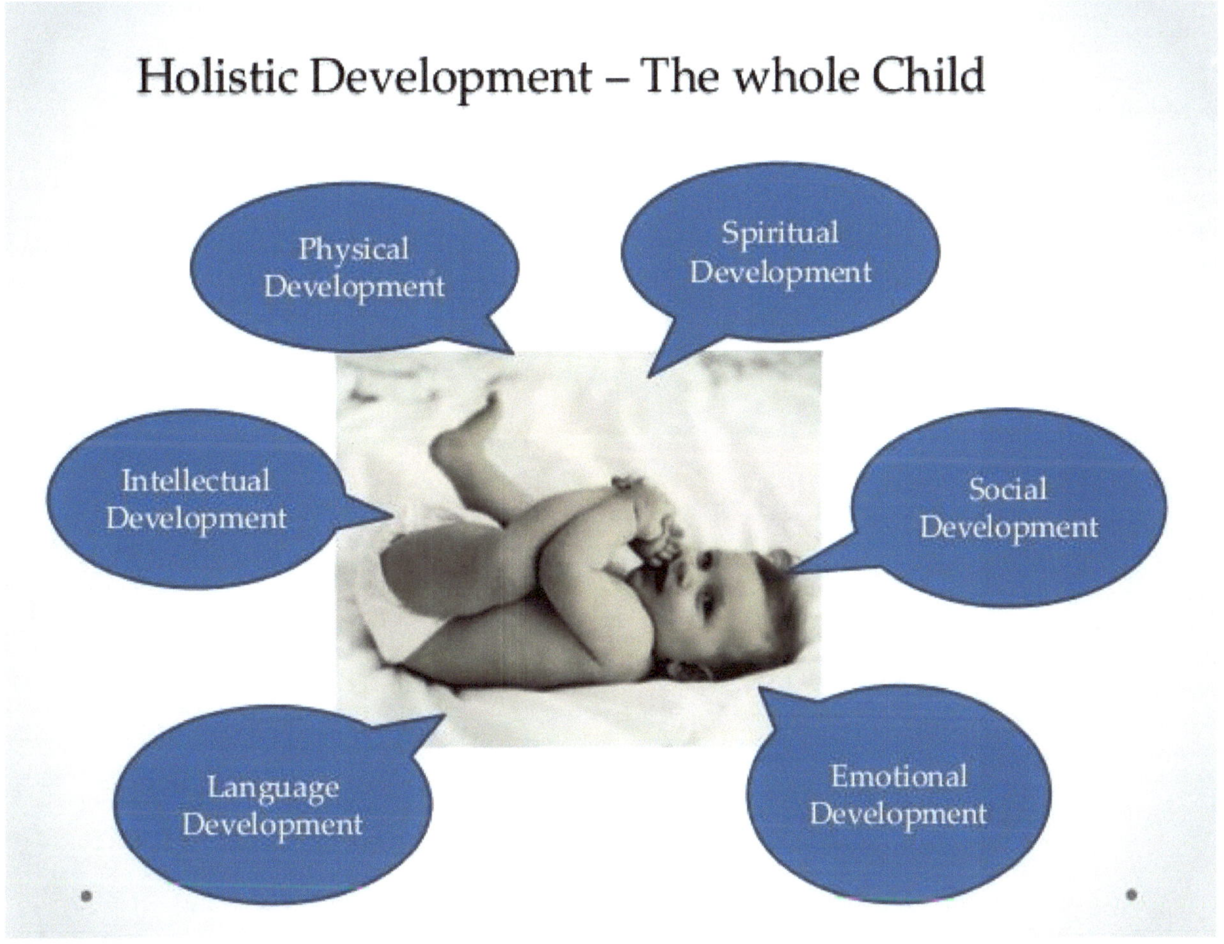

(Google Image)

The first approach to tackling early childhood is to take a holistic approach to child development.

What is Holistic Child Development?

Holistic child development is taking a whole or complete approach to child development. It consists of the acronyms PILESS:

P: Physical

I: Intellectual/Cognitive

L: Language

E: Emotional

S: Social

S: Spiritual

Holistic development concentrates on the overall development of the child: physical, intellectual/cognitive, language, emotional, social, and spiritual aspects. In the area of early childhood, there is a need for child development to be holistic.

Physical Child Development

This is the children's ability to use their fine, gross motor skills and hand eye coordination. Fine motor skills are when children use their fingertips, while gross motor skills are when children use their whole body/large muscles in the body (bodily movement).

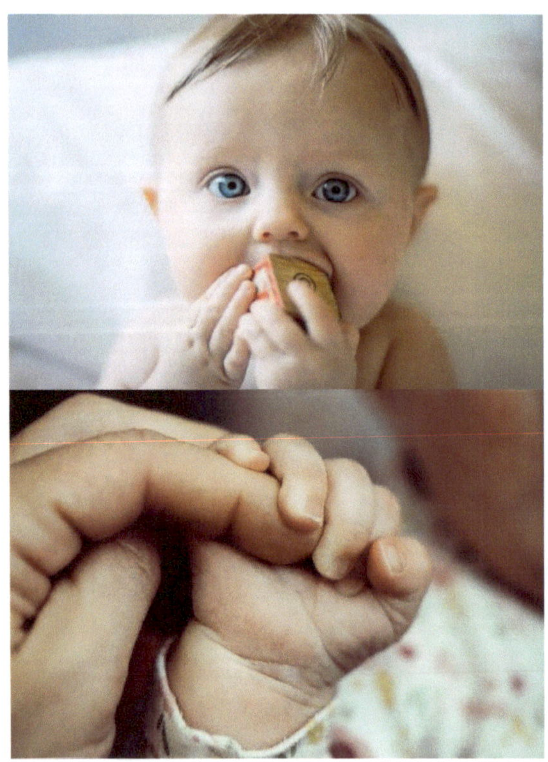

Intellectual/Cognitive Child Development

This is the development of the mind (mental and cognitive development), when children think, process information, use their imagination, recognise, reason, know, understand, and develop ideas.

Language Child Development

This is the ability of the child to communicate in terms of verbal and non-verbal communication. It also has to do with children's abilities to listen, express themselves by using words, facial expressions, such as smiling, laughing, crying, hand gestures, and many more.

Emotional Child Development

This is when children can control their feelings. It also has to do with children's abilities to express their feelings, such as happiness, fear, anger, frustration, contentment, worry in positive ways.

Social Child Development

This is the process where children learn skills and attitudes that enable them to live easily with people in their community. This also has to do with children's abilities to interact with people (adults, peers, family members) and things around them.

Spiritual Child Development

There is a need to recognise that spiritual understanding, thoughts, and feelings are as much a part of the growth process for children as their physical, intellectual, language, emotional or social development. Most importantly, children began to search for this from a young age when they can think abstractly.

Spiritual development is defined as part of the child's inner being through which they experience the interactions of their values, emotions and beliefs with each other and their relationship to a divine being. It begins when children can first frame the question 'why.'

How can you promote holistic child development?

The goal of early childhood education is to focus on holistic child development, and to promote holistic child development, child observation is the key. Child observation brings to light children's interests, strengths and needs. This is the first and best approach to holistic child development. Activities will need to be mapped out to promote children's holistic development from the information gathered from child observations.

Physical Development:

Children could be encouraged to use their fine motor skills (fingertips), gross motor skills (whole body) and hand eye coordination through the following ways:

- Children's physical growth must be nourished through healthy foods, such as fruits, water, proteins (fish, eggs, meat), cereals, mashed potatoes, rice, beans, and many more.
- Construction of Lego, jigsaws, playdough
- Painting, colouring, drawing, cutting/slicing with plastic scissors/knives, handwriting/writing.
- Mark making, book making, handprints and footprints.
- Books flipping/grasping and also opportunities for children to feel the textures of books.
- Pointing/Pouring/Scooping/Mixing/Shaking
- Climbing/Throwing/Catching/Kicking
- Children should be encouraged to use spoons, knives, and forks (under adult supervision)
- Clapping/Dancing/singing of action songs
- Jumping/Jogging/Hopping/Skipping/Running
- Going for a walk/nature walk
- Allow children to open letter/mailbox/lunch boxes.
- Allow children to pick up things from the floors, such as toys, plates, spoons, clothes, shoes, pencils, balls, books.

Intellectual/Cognitive Development

- Ask children meaningful questions.
- Present children with interesting and enjoyable things to do, such as make and create things (make cards, storybooks, picture books)
- Present children with choice of meaningful experiences
- Observe children's thinking and document the ideas they develop.
- Adapt experiences to suit children's needs and interests.

- Create opportunities for children to talk, play and play with others, such as their peers, family members and teachers.
- Encourage children to practice new skills, such as dressing themselves, drawing, playing games, and many more.
- Place children in positions where they can see what is going on around them.
- Encourage children to use books to increase their knowledge and awareness.
- Provide children with objects and toys that will encourage them to concentrate, investigate and stimulate their imagination.
- Encourage children to listen to stories to boost their listening and concentration skills.
- Provide children with opportunities for discovery by promoting their curiosity and exploring new places with them.

Language Development

- Create a conducive environment that promotes language development.
- Follow the lead of the child.
- Copy what the child is doing verbally and non-verbally.
- Read books to children.
- Encourage children to express themselves using words and facial expressions.
- Engage children in meaningful conversations.
- Encourage children to read books.
- Read to your unborn child: this will expose your unborn child to words.
- Sing nursery rhymes and encourage repetition.
- Encourage children to practise making sounds (babbling)
- Practice listening and speaking with the children.
- Allow children to copy sounds made by other people.
- Encourage children to learn what sounds mean.
- Encourage children to pronounce words.
- Ask children open-ended questions and wait for their answers.

 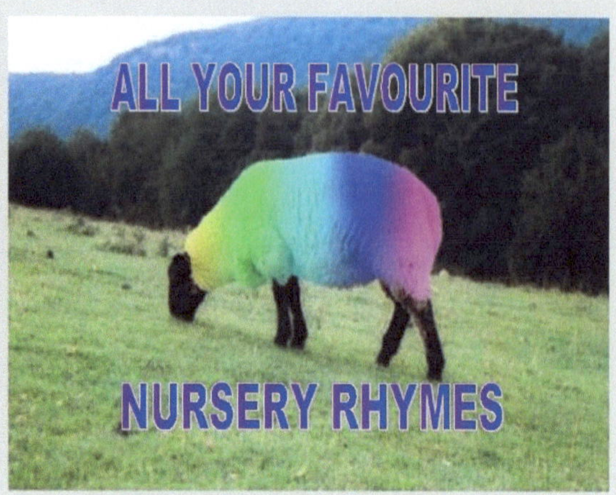

Emotional Development

- Encourage children to express their feelings in positive ways.
- Talk about feelings with children.
- Read books on feelings and emotions and discuss these with the children.
- Encourage children to represent their emotions through drawing pictures.
- Channel children's energy to positive things
- Reinforce positive behaviours when children display this. This will strengthen future positive emotions.
- Give children a break and encourage them to do what they like (go for a walk, take a deep breath, listen to music to relieve stress, anger, and tension)
- Build a strong relationship with children built on love and trust.
- Create a loving, comfortable and supportive environment where children can learn and grow.
- Offer empathy and encouragement to children.

Social Development

- Engage children in interactive activities.
- Encourage activities that bring children into the company of other people, both inside and outside the home
- Teach children to learn how to share, take turns and accept rules.
- Encourage children to mix, meet and communicate with others.
- Encourage children to eat in a manner that does not offend others.
- Teach children standards of cleanliness that is acceptable in the society.
- Encourage children to show empathy and respect for others.
- Listen to and encourage children to also listen to you.
- Encourage children to make friendships.
- Encourage children to engage in structured group play (play with a purpose), such as board game, Simon says, peek-a-boo.

- Firstly, you need to admit you do not know everything about spirituality and seek to expand your own knowledge on this subject matter.
- Encourage children to express their thoughts or question religious values without becoming judgmental.
- Treat children's questions about spiritual matters with utmost respect.
- Recognise children's innate feelings.
- Engage children in informal discussions about spirituality.

(Google Image)

Remember, children must learn these skills, and it is your role to teach them, and if you do not teach them, how will they learn?

In conclusion, the holistic development of children in the context of early childhood education needs to be recognised and valued by all.

Challenging behaviour is a term used to describe how a child acts that interferes with his/her daily life. Examples of challenging behaviours in young children are hitting, biting, kicking, aggressiveness, non-cooperation, unwillingness to share, spitting, and many more.

Young children present with challenging behaviour for some of these reasons: to express a want, seek the attention of adults or other people in their environment, tiredness during the day, too much going on around their environment, such as too much light, noisy areas, need for stimulation, for example, teething, which could sometimes lead to biting.

Young children also present with challenging behaviour to express anger and frustration. However, it is normal for young children to present with challenging behaviour, but they do need to learn to use other means to express what they want.

- You must be calm whenever young children present with challenging behaviour.
- You must take a deep breath and not make a scene of the situation at hand.
- You do not need to shout when young children present with challenging behaviour like most people do and remember behaviours that young children bring up; the responses are either negative or positive.
- Do not focus too much on this behaviour. It is important to note that the calmer you address the child, the quicker they will calm down, but you must maintain a firm and strong voice to teach young children discipline while at the same time, teach them that a calm and maintained character is best in difficult situations.
- When young children start to present with challenging behaviours, you must teach them the skills they need to interact and express their emotions.
- You must teach your children to use words to express their emotions. For example, you could say to the child to use phrases such as 'I am not happy because Temi took away my toy.' 'I am sad because Mary is not playing

with me,' 'I am cross because my brother Johnny took my pen.' The list is ongoing.

- You must constantly remind young children to express their feelings but not by being aggressive.
- Constant reminders could be achieved by having rules around how young children could express their emotions.

- You could have rules, such as 'We speak out when our friends hurt us,' 'We play nicely with our friends,' 'We share our toys with everyone.' This is important, as it will help to remind young children to express their feelings rather than acting out.
- You could also create a visual schedule/timetable of day-to-day activities as some young children might display challenging behaviour when they are unsure of what will happen next in their environment.

- Creating a schedule of the day's activities will show young children what they will be doing throughout the day and when.

Visual Aid Template

- You must learn prevention techniques, ("prevention is better than cure"). You must map out ways that challenging behaviours could be prevented before they occur. Sometimes, most of the challenging behaviours that young children present with can be avoided before it even happens.
- You must observe what triggers such challenging behaviours and try your possible best to remove these. For instance, two children could be playing with a toy, and you observe that after a while, they start to drag the toy. You need to immediately step in as an adult to offer solutions on how the children could take turns to play with the toy.
- You could suggest a child play with the toy first for few minutes while the other child waits their turn to play with the toy. This will help to prevent challenging behaviour from occurring, and at the same time, you are teaching them to wait their turn.
- You must redirect the child's attention to something positive, such as playing or learning, essentially providing them with a distraction. When you do this, the child will learn to channel their energy to something productive and beneficial.
- For example, if you observed that a young child with challenging behaviour loved to go on nature walk, you could distract this child by bringing him on a nature walk when he starts to present with challenging behaviour. You could also shift the focus of the young child by reading him a story, allowing the child to pick the book.
- Check your environment and reduce what might be causing challenging behaviour. For example, you could reduce the lighting, the noise level, and the activities going on in the environment, as young children might be overwhelmed by these.
- You need to have a discussion around how to prevent these challenging behaviours with young children.
- Books could be useful in this area. Buy books and use them to teach your children how to express themselves instead of presenting with challenging behaviours.
- You could try reward charts, as this will enable young children to visually see their positive behaviour over the course of the day or week.

- You need to understand that encouraging young children to change a behaviour can be tricky, but reward charts can be a powerful way of kickstarting that change. Reward charts come in several forms, such as wall posters and apps.
- Reward charts name or show a positive behaviour or goal you want young children to achieve. A certain number of ticks, stickers or starts adds up to a reward for the children.

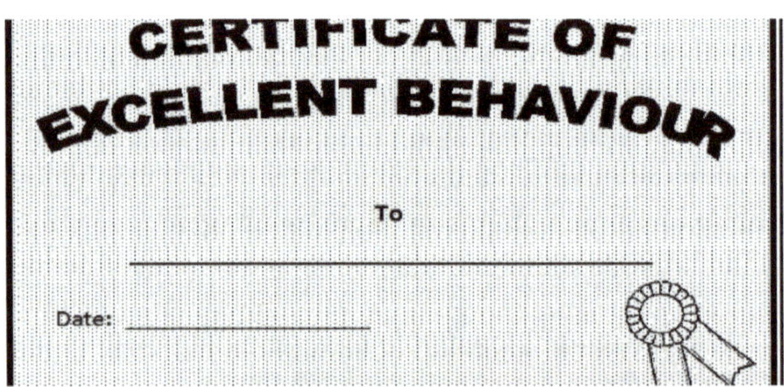

	Reinforcement (Increase / maintain behavior)	Punishment (Decrease behavior)
Positive (add stimulus)	**Add** pleasant stimulus *to* **Increase / maintain** behavior	**Add** aversive stimulus *to* **Decrease** behavior
Negative (remove stimulus)	**Remove** aversive stimulus *to* **Increase / maintain** behavior	**Remove** pleasant stimulus *to* **Decrease** behavior

- Give the reward to the child or children at the end of the behaviour set goal, as this will encourage the behaviour you want to see in the child/children to occur more.
- Try to focus on young children rather than the challenging behaviour they present and remember, the goal of early years is to nurture young children to be unique individuals and boost their self-esteem.
- Give young children a balanced diet and cut down on screen time to help find out if there may be a link between food and behaviour.
- Finally, do not forget to manage your own stress. You need to wind down after dealing with challenging situations. You could do this through the following ways: play music, go for walks, dance, cook, engage in sports (running, jumping, swimming), singing, and many more. Most importantly, do what makes you feel good and replenished after dealing with young children's challenging behaviours.

Mathematics plays a major role in child development, and it helps children makes sense of the world around them. It is important that we develop early mathematical skills in young children, as they will need these skills  later in life, perhaps when they go into primary schools, become teenagers and adults themselves. Mathematical skills are needed for every day-to-day activity. Young children becoming familiar with their routines, such as brushing their teeth, feeding, getting dressed, taking a nap, going shopping, playing can all become math learning opportunities when approached in certain ways.

- Ways you could promote early mathematical skills in young children

- Ask children to identify colours and shapes in their environment. For example, 'Johnny, what colour is your book?' 'Tammy, what colour is your jumper?' 'Anum what colour is your shoes?' 'Dara, what colour is your water bottle?' 'Divine, what shape is your bowl?' 'Nife, what shape is your storybook?' 'Gracey, what shape is the TV?' 'Tony, what shape is our oven?' Deji, what shape is your school bag?' 'Bunmi, what shape is our fridge?' Demmy, what shape is this table?'

- For more than one child, you could say, 'Can anyone identify the square shape?' 'Can anyone identify the colour purple?' 'Can anyone identify the blue shape?' 'Can anyone identity the green shape from the kitchen area?' and many more.

- Using the I spy game to identify colours and shapes in the environment with young children.

- Children learn through play, so using the I spy game will encourage young children to participate in this game. In return, they are learning about shapes and colours, and at the same time, socialising with people around them. For example, 'I spy with my little eye something that is pink,' 'I spy with my little eye something that is yellow.'

- You could also take the I spy game further by being specific. 'I spy with my little eye something that is blue in the kitchen area,' 'I spy with my little eye something that is black in the bathroom,' 'I spy with my little eye something that is green in the living room,' 'I spy with my little eye something that is purple in the car,' 'I spy with my little eye something that is orange in this park,' 'I spy with my little eye something that is white outside the window,'

- Encourage children to look at pictures to develop an awareness of colours, shapes, sizes and numbers of objects.
- Sing songs that have rhymes, shapes, and numbers with young children. Songs such as:

12345 Once I caught a fish Alive

One, two, three, four, five,
Once I caught a fish alive,
Six, seven, eight, nine, ten,
Then I let it go again.

Why did you let it go?
Because it bit my finger so.
Which finger did it bite?
This little finger on the right.

Alphabet Song (Abc's)

A B C D E F G
H I J K L M N O P
Q R S T U V
W X Y and Z

Now I know my ABCs
Next time won't you sing with me.

Baa Baa Black Sheep

Baa, baa black sheep
Have you any wool
Yes sir, yes sir
Three bags full.

One for the master
And one for the dame
And one for the little boy
Who lives down the lane.

Humpty Dumpty

Humpty Dumpty sat on a wall,
Humpty Dumpty had a great fall.
All the King's horses and all the King's men,
Couldn't put Humpty together again.

I'm a Little Teapot

I'm a little teapot
Short and stout
Here is my handle
Here is my spout.

When I get all steamed up
Hear me shout
"Tip me over
and pour me out!'.

- These songs will encourage children to identity patterns.
- Encourage children to cut fruits, such as bananas, apples, oranges, avocados, kiwis into some shapes and count together. This should be done in a fun way to encourage children to develop early mathematical skills.
- During play time, encourage children to mix, pour, scoop sand/water together.
- Ask children to count how many steps it will take them to move from the kitchen area to the living room, how many steps will it take from the

bathroom to the guest room. You could combine these with the children to make it fun.

- Going on a walk with the children to the local park, bus station, train station, local shops and count how many steps it will take you and the children to get to these places.
- Ask children to sort out their toys. For example, 'Johnny, put all your red toys together,' 'Johnny, can you gather all your blue and green toys into the black sack please.'
- Some common play items, such as peg number boards, playdough, jigsaw puzzles, counting bears, and many more, can be used as tools to help teach fundamental math skills like adding and subtracting.
- Painting and colouring could also help children to develop mathematical skills, such as learning about colours and shapes.

You need to remember that maths skills taught in early childhood education lay the foundation for children to succeed in primary school and beyond.

Independent learning skills are skills that young children will need to solve a problem, experience a situation or a challenge. It is vital that young children develop independent learning skills, as they will need these skills later in life.

Note: Sometimes, you do too much for young children without realising that these children have the skills to do things when prompted to do so.

Practical ways to develop independence learning skills in young children

- Encourage children to feed themselves from an early stage.
- Encourage children to tie their shoelaces, canvas laces, trainer laces.
- Encourage children to wear their shoes, socks, coats, aprons, hand gloves, hats, caps, shirt, dress, trousers, pyjamas, jackets, the list is ongoing.
- Encourage children to button/zip their clothes.
- Ask children to tidy up after themselves after every meal and snack time.
- Ask children to bring their bowls, plates, spoons, forks, the list is ongoing, to the sink area.
- Ask children to help with simple household chores, such as getting milk, butter, honey from the fridge, the list is ongoing.
- Ask children to put their dirty clothes into the laundry basket.
- Ask children to sort their socks, clothes, the list is ongoing.
- Ask children to tidy up after play.
- Ask children to carry their school bags, get your mobile phone, television remote, laptops, packer and sweeping brush.
- Allow children to pick a storybook of their choice, choose the painting of their choice, choose the types of toys they want to play with, and many more.
- Allow young children to brush their teeth under adult supervision (show and tell).
- Allow children to assist with simple tasks, such as getting the cooking pots, spoons, and many more when you are preparing meals in the kitchen.
- Allow children to come with ideas when you are making the shopping lists.
- Allow children to wash their hands independently.
- Allow children to construct their own play with little input from the adults.

Timing is important when you want to develop independent learning skills in young children. You need to give sufficient time for young children to achieve the tasks that you want them to do and remember to always give positive reinforcement, such as 'Well done,' 'Thank you for helping to tidy up,' 'You did well tying your shoes laces yourself' after every task completed by young children. This will boost young children's self-esteem in terms of what they were able to achieve by themselves without any help.

Remember, you need to step back and allow young children do things for themselves, and you will be amazed by what they can do without your help.

'We are different, we are unique individuals in our own way.'

Diversity consists of a quality that make individuals different. It is what makes us unique in our own way. Children's individual interests and capabilities, racial and cultural differences, age and gender difference and language differences play a part in *diversity*. *Diversity* should be taught starting from *Early Childhood*.

Diversity has to do with young children having knowledge about people in the world, about diversity and equality.

Young children must be taught from a younger age to acknowledge that diversity exists and also see that this difference is what makes everyone unique.

Children must know that we are all different, and that is what makes us special. Positive role models are important when you want to teach children about diversity. You must lead by example by respecting differences and lay the foundation to build on fostering kindness and respect for all (you cannot give what you do not have).

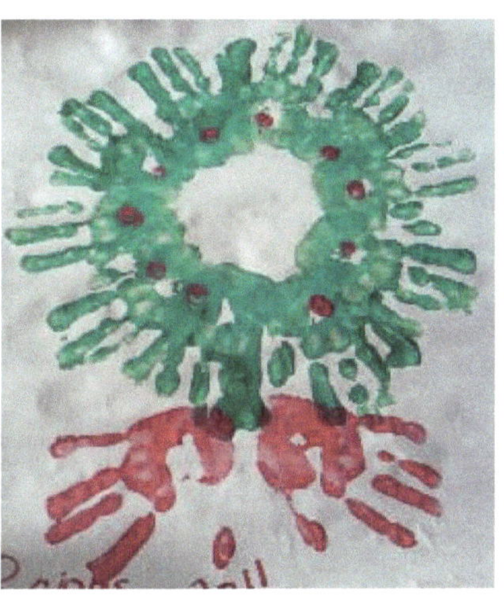

Ways to teach children about diversity

- The approach to teaching young children about diversity is to know that it starts from you. You need to be accepting, as young children imitate people around them. You need to examine your own beliefs and query your own biases.
- Include food of different culture in your menus. Explain these foods to children and encourage them to try these foods.
- Have toys that reflect different culture, age, gender, abilities. Talk and comment on these toys and motivate young children to play with them.

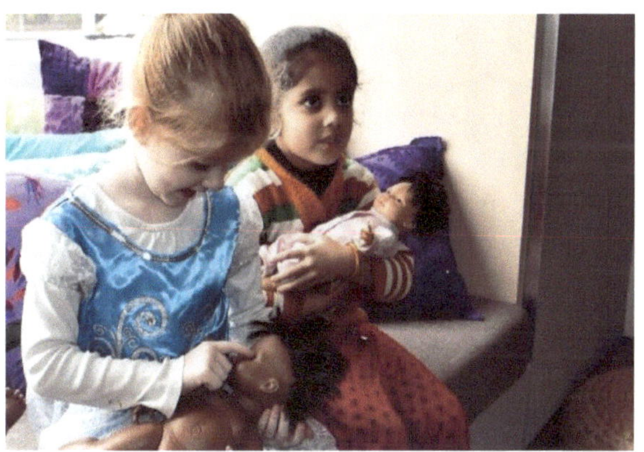

- Read books that represent different backgrounds, different religions, family structures, abilities, strengths with young children.
- Talk about diversity and encourage young children to ask questions on diversities.
- Play music from different backgrounds for children to listen to and remember, inclusion is the key.
- Provide children with paints of different colours to use and see that differences exists.

- Discuss the globe with children using the world map.

- Encourage Questions: Whenever young children have questions about differences in physical characteristics or cultural practices, discuss them openly. This teaches children that it is okay to notice differences, and more importantly, it teaches them that it is good to talk about these differences.

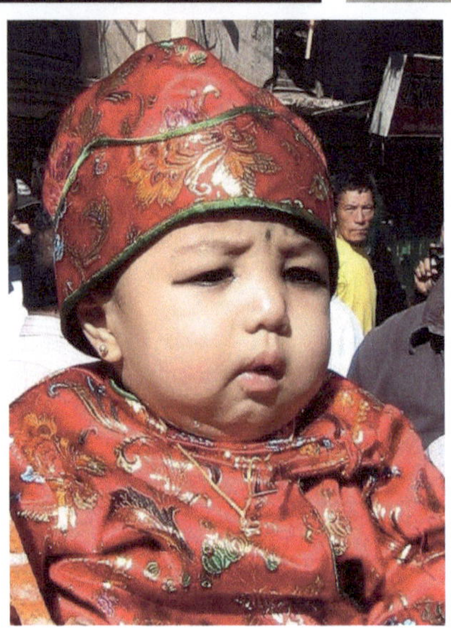 

- Use various cultures to inspire holiday decorations.
- Attend cultural events and discuss these with children.
- Watch movies, such as Jungle Book, Aladdin, and many more that introduce new places to raise global awareness.
- Use posters, games, puzzles, stories and rhymes that represent diversity and discuss these with children.

- Include resources that portray children with positive role models.
- Provide an inclusive environment, where all children will feel love, respect, learn, and grow together.

In conclusion, you must consider the similarities and differences when discussing diversity with young children and remember to ensure these are discussed in positive ways to promote inclusion.

www.ingramcontent.com/pod-product-compliance
Lightning Source LLC
Chambersburg PA
CBHW042009110726
48006CB00004B/1021